oh my soul

ENCOUNTERING GOD

IN HONEST, UNCONVENTIONAL

(AND SOMETIMES MESSY)

PRAYER

DEVOTIONAL

shannon guerra

Scripture quotations are from the ESV® Bible (The Holy Bible, English Standard Version®), copyright © 2001 by Crossway, a publishing ministry of Good News Publishers. Used by permission. All rights reserved.

Some excerpts taken from *Oh My Soul: Encountering God in Honest, Unconventional (and Sometimes Messy) Prayer*, copyright © 2018 by Shannon Guerra.

ISBN 978-1-7345978-8-2

Cover art by Kelly Bermudez, Willow Lief Design Co.

This title may be purchased in bulk for educational or group study use. For more information, please email shop@copperlightwood.com.

Printed and bound in the United States of America

Published by Copperlight Wood
P.O. Box 870697
Wasilla, AK
99687
 www.copperlightwood.com

contents

HELLO.

If there was **one thing** I could do that would always, without fail, make me stronger and wiser, would I do it?

What if doing that one thing always made me more **whole and healed and at peace** than I was the day before, and at the same time, it transformed the world around me? Would I do it more often?

If there was something I could do that would **cause me to win every time,** how often would I do it?

I'd do it all the time. I'd do it without ceasing.

And this is what happens when we encounter God, and live in His presence, in continual conversation with Him.

WAYS TO USE THIS STUDY

Lite: Just a few minutes a day.

- Just read the study. Then talk to God about it.
- Notice how He speaks to you (and how you speak to Him) through the rest of the day.

Medium: 15-20 minutes a day. Add the following:

- Copy the scriptures in here, or copy them onto a few sticky notes, and put them in strategic places so you can read them throughout the day.
- Pick one of the questions to journal through.
- Read one-third of the corresponding chapter from *Oh My Soul* each day.

Going deep, for personal use or a group study: 30-60 minutes per session. Add the following:

- Discuss/journal through all of the questions.
- Work through one-third of the corresponding chapter in the *Oh My Soul Companion Journal*.

DAY 1

ABIDING

Oh My Soul is just a record of me learning to hear God and learning to pray without ceasing, written to encourage you on your own journey of learning to hear God and learning to pray without ceasing.

Ephesians 6:16-18 says:

> *In all circumstances take up the shield of faith, with which you can extinguish all the flaming darts of the evil one; and take the helmet of salvation, and the sword of the Spirit, which is the word of God, praying at all times in the Spirit, with all prayer and supplication. To that end keep alert with all perseverance, making supplication for all the saints.*

Supplication is just a fancy word for "asking."

And I asked God to teach me to pray without ceasing.

You can file it under either "the abundantly generous nature of God" or "be careful what you ask for" – take your pick – because in spite of only asking Him about unceasing prayer, He was aggravatingly thorough. He insisted on teaching me about grit, surrender, confession, repentance, brokenness, fear, friendship, shame, hope, procrastination, identity, routine, and healing.

Mostly, it was just Him and me talking in the off-moments. I need to hear His thoughts in normal days, in grey days, in dark days, to steward my life well. We're still talking. I'm still learning.

Sometimes we err in thinking that prayer needs to be refined, holy sounding, and set aside for remote, quiet places where no one goes – like the woods, or, let's be honest, a neighborhood HOA meeting. But, no. Nope, not at all.

Prayer needs to be right here with us in the joy and mess of everyday life because this is where we need Him: in these moments of office meetings, running errands, helping customers and coworkers, scrubbing stained carpet, and teaching our kids math (especially that). Our conversation with God is constantly interrupted, and yet, not so – because He's right there, unoffended by the activity of daily life.

Learning to hear Him changes everything.

Disasters averted, hearts healed, people saved, dreams realized.

Missions accomplished.

And you and I, we're here walking through all of our days, partnering with Him in ways that bring life and make the darkness flee. Outwardly, we're on our feet, eyes open – inwardly, we're on our knees, eyes up.

questions to consider:

- What is the hardest thing about praying without ceasing?
- Why do we forget to abide?
- What distracts you from abiding?

(more) scripture for today:

> *...until the Spirit is poured upon us from on high,*
> *and the wilderness becomes a fruitful field,*
> *and the fruitful field is deemed a forest.*
> *Then justice will dwell in the wilderness,*
> *and righteousness abide in the fruitful field.*
> *And the effect of righteousness will be peace,*
> *and the result of righteousness,*
> *quietness and trust forever.*
> *My people will abide in a peaceful habitation,*
> *in secure dwellings, and in quiet resting places.*
>
> *- Isaiah 32:15-18*

_____

_____

_____

_____

_____

_____

_____

_____

_____

_____

DAY 2

ABIDING

Much of what eventually became *Oh My Soul* came from a couple of 31-day series about praying without ceasing. I did it two years in a row – same topic, different titles, all new written content. The night before the launch of one of those series, I was puttering around with a photo editing program, redoing all of my graphics because it was the most productive way to procrastinate I could think of.

I put the new graphics into the post and proceeded to methodically type out "day 1," "day 2," "day 3," and on and on, which was a wonderful, non-thinking autopilot activity until I got to day 31. And then there was nothing left to do, but write.

And I did write – for about 98 words, until I got stuck trying to figure out an illustration. I needed some ideas. And I thought to myself, *Let us consult Pinterest.*

It was all in the name of research, of course. Thanks to my commitment to learning about prayer, I'd hardly even peeked at the opiates – I mean, opportunities – on there.

I knew I should be writing, or doing the dishes, or at the very least, getting the cat off the counter where she was hunting for leftover scraps of dinner, but there might...be something amazing...if I scrolled...a little farther...

BAM. A recipe for one of my favorite cookies that uses only three ingredients. Told you.

Charles Spurgeon once said, "The worst thing that can happen to a gambler is to win," and he's right, because upon further investigation I discovered that one of the "ingredients" was a commercially-made cookie consisting of 38 chemicals that looked similar to what I've seen on labels of laundry detergent. So it wasn't a win for me; it was a disappointment.

And the Spirit said to me, *What did you expect?*

And I said, *Well, with only three ingredients...I guess I was hoping for a miracle.*

And He said, Well, Love, you were looking in the wrong place for that, weren't you? (Did you know the Spirit will sass you back sometimes?)

I moved on, and after forty-five minutes I finally figured out what I needed for the illustration, which seems like an unimpressive return on my investment. But I also pinned six things, read three articles, and firmly rejected the idea of painting all of the doors in our house aqua.

It's not just our distractible nature that is roving. God is moving among us as we go about the hours of our day.

Hey, Love, He told me, *when you're bored and scrolling without purpose, looking for inspiration and not finding it, it's time to look in different direction. Your time with Me will never disappoint you. I will always leave you wiser, or rested, or both. You don't want to miss this.*

This time with God is bountiful, potent, and effective to change and restore anything you are avoiding. This time is fertile to bring forth what you are waiting for. This time creates prolific momentum toward everything you are working for. This time with God is never a gamble.

You will always gain. You will always bear fruit. You will always find peace when you encounter Him. You will always win when you spend time with God.

Our awareness of His presence allows Him to come between us and our agendas, and He is with us at the desk with our computers, at the table with our kids, and with us when we sleep. His peace is for you, for me, every second.

questions to consider:

- What do you do when you realize you haven't been abiding?
- Do you struggle with feeling condemnation, shame, or feeling "out of favor" when you realize you haven't been abiding?
- What helps you return quickly?

scripture for today:

> *There is therefore now no condemnation for those who are in Christ Jesus. For the law of the Spirit of life has set you free in Christ Jesus from the law of sin and death.*
> *- Romans 8:1-2*

> *But seek first the kingdom of God and his righteousness, and all these things will be added to you.*
> *- Matthew 6:33*

_____

_____

_____

_____

_____

_____

_____

DAY 3

ABIDING

I once read a book about someone who was restoring an old house, and the author caught herself on the word "abide."

And there's an incredible relationship between these words "**abide**" and "**restore**."

We abide in our homes, and when we love the homes we live in, we can't help but make a restorative impact on them: We make repairs, we make improvements, we decorate. **We make it ours.** We make an impact on the function, strength, and beauty of the place we abide in.

This is what the Spirit does when we abide with Him.

We abide, but He is also abiding in us. When we recognize His presence in our own abiding – we invite Him into all our spaces – He makes an impact on the function, strength, and beauty of our life. He does it because He loves it here. And that love restores us. He makes us His.

Abiding is rest, not striving. Not stressing, not impressing, not trying to prove ourselves. It is loving the place we're in, because He is the place we're in. It is looking to Him as the shelter, and not the physical stuff or circumstances around us.

And the real miracle is that when we abide in Him, He abides right back in us. He makes us His home, and starts rearranging everything in the best way.

In the following sections, we'll continue to talk about abiding, since that's how we encounter God. If there's no abiding, there's no praying without ceasing.

But we'll also go over topics like identity, our dreams, and the boldness to walk in obedience toward those dreams in spite of fear and other spiritual attacks. We'll talk about friendship and the role it plays in our spiritual growth. And we'll look at intercession, and how we transform and make an impact on the culture around us.

In the next section we'll go over **identity**, which also involves fun things like repentance, surrender, maturity, and finding freedom from shame. It's the hard-but-necessary foundational stuff that clears the way for breakthrough.

And there's breakthrough ahead. The victory is here.

The comfort or discomfort of our outward lives depends more largely upon the dwelling place of our bodies than upon almost any other material thing; and the comfort or discomfort of our inward life depends similarly upon the dwelling place of our souls....It is of vital importance, then, that we should find out definitely where our souls are living. The Lord declares that He has been our dwelling place in all generations, but the question is, Are we living in our dwelling place? ....Our Lord Himself urges this invitation upon us. "Abide in Me," He says, "and I in you"; and He goes on to tell us what are the blessed results of this abiding, and what are the sad consequences of not abiding.

The truth is, our souls were made for God.

He is our natural home, and we can never be at rest anywhere else.

- Hannah Whitall Smith [1]

questions to consider:

- What routines can help you stay in the rhythm of abiding?
- How does abiding create rest in our days?
- Can you describe a season in your life when you were abiding well? What did it look like?

scripture for today:

I will extol you, my God and King,
and bless your name forever and ever.
Every day I will bless you and praise your name
forever and ever.
Great is the Lord, and greatly to be praised,
and his greatness is unsearchable.
One generation shall commend your works to another,
and shall declare your mighty acts.
On the glorious splendor of your majesty,
and on your wondrous works, I will meditate.
- Psalm 145:1-5

_____

_____

_____

DAY 4

IDENTITY

Our identities can be pretty complicated.

There's the stuff we know about ourselves (the truth), the stuff we believe about ourselves (which may or may not be true), and then there's stuff that we've convinced ourselves of to make ourselves feel better (which is not true, or only partly true). And *then* there's the stuff that God knows about us – the complete picture, the whole truth.

It can take us a long time to discover things about ourselves. Why do certain things trigger us? Why do other things light us up? Why do some things from our past still rile us up, even though we thought they were taken care of long ago?

Here's a personal example. A while back, I showed up for a meeting – one that I go to regularly. But instead of finding the meeting I expected, I found myself at a party I was not invited to. No one had notified me that the meeting was changed, though it was obvious that everyone else in the room knew.

My role there is different, and communicating the change to me fell through the cracks. Someone dropped the ball. It happens.

I tried to play it off, but I went home far more upset than I felt I should've been, and that made me even more upset. I felt completely rejected, overlooked, and devalued.

Why all these feelings?

I wrestled with God over it, trying to figure out why I felt so bad over a simple miscommunication. He reminded me of things I overcame in my childhood, things I thought I'd dealt with long ago:

I grew up in a broken home, constantly going back and forth between my parents' houses, never feeling like I belonged to either of them. Never really fit in with either family. The lies I overcame from those experiences were, *You don't belong, you're not one of us. You're too different and you never fit in with other people. You're not like everyone else. This stuff isn't for you, it's for the people who belong here – and you're not one of them.*

It took me a while that day to recognize what the enemy was doing and how he was using my past to hurt me and create offense. He was trying to bring a wedge into important relationships, and get me to believe things about myself (and others) that weren't true.

2 Corinthians 3:17 says:

Where the Spirit of the Lord is, there is freedom.

When we make a point of taking those things that hurt and hold them up to God, He shows us what is going on under the surface and He tells us what is true.

He brings freedom.

And *that* is our identity.

questions to consider:

- Describe a situation when you realized the truth about a lie you'd believed about yourself or your past.
- What beliefs do you have about your identity that might not be true?
- What current situation could you hold up to God and ask Him to bring truth and freedom in?

(more) scripture for today:

> *From now on, therefore, we regard no one according to the flesh. Even though we once regarded Christ according to the flesh, we regard him thus no longer.*
>
> *Therefore, if anyone is in Christ, he is a new creation.*
>
> *The old has passed away; behold, the new has come.*
>
> *All this is from God, who through Christ reconciled us to himself and gave us the ministry of reconciliation.*
>
> *- 2 Corinthians 5:16-18*

_____

_____

_____

_____

_____

_____

_____

_____

DAY 5

IDENTITY

A few years ago I was talking with one of our kids about a particular privilege he wanted. He was asking me, "Why can't I have *xyz* yet?"

"Because you still have those things you haven't taken care of yet," I answered. "And you need to apologize to your sister and brother for that other situation, too."

I actually really wanted him to have xyz. I wanted him to have the whole crazy alphabet. I didn't want to lay a heavy burden on him, and I didn't want him to feel defeated at every turn. But he'd been making things hard on himself by piling up outstanding relational debt, so I laid it out there.

And he said, "I'm sorry. I'm sorry for that one situation."

"Thanks...I forgive you," I said, and waited to see if he would take responsibility for the rest. But he didn't. And the business remained unfinished. And he never did get xyz.

Undealt with, these situations are like pieces of grit building up in a pipe. If they're not irrigated quickly, they cement themselves in like so many embedded rocks. Eventually the choice to let things calcify becomes a habit, and our lives that are meant to be conduits are blocked entirely.

The Spirit can't flow through when we refuse to deal with the muck.

Galatians 5:7 says:

> **You were running well.** *Who hindered you from obeying the truth?*

Resentment, bitterness, unforgiveness, and refusal to accept responsibility hinder our effectiveness in prayer. They are rocks we trip over, boulders we butt up against, and we wonder why our prayers seem to go nowhere. Sometimes it's because we've let things pile up, and they've cemented right in the middle of our path.

But they don't have to stay there.

James 5:16 says:

> *Therefore, confess your sins to one another and pray for one another, that you may be healed. The prayer of a righteous person has great power as it is working.*

Humility and repentance are the gentle dynamite that clears our path. It's not that God doesn't hear us, or doesn't want xyz and the rest of the whole crazy alphabet for us. Sometimes, we've got some unfinished business to attend to first.

It's highly virtuous to say we'll be good, but we can't do it all at once, and it takes a long pull, a strong pull, and a pull all together, before some of us even get our feet set in the right way.

- Louisa May Alcott [2]

questions to consider:

- Has God been prompting you to deal with something that you've been avoiding?
- What does the first step to dealing with that look like?
- What is waiting for you on the other side of obedience?

(more) scripture for today:

The saying is trustworthy and deserving of full acceptance, that Christ Jesus came into the world to save sinners, of whom I am the foremost. But I received mercy for this reason, that in me, as the foremost, Jesus Christ might display his perfect patience as an example to those who were to believe in him for eternal life.

To the King of the ages, immortal, invisible, the only God, be honor and glory forever and ever. Amen.

- 1 Timothy 1:15-17

_____

_____

_____

_____

_____

_____

_____

_____

DAY 6

IDENTITY

Why is simple obedience so hard sometimes? Why is it so hard for us to leave our old patterns and ways, even when we know they're costing us?

The Spirit reminded me that shame, fear, and control are merciless task-masters.

He said, *People are afraid of changing because they fear future shame, not understanding there is no shame in repentance. It's the enemy's ruse to keep them from growing closer to Me. They only need to ask to be excused, and My grace covers them. Because healing comes in the closeness.*

So we consider our options. And sometimes we wonder...If we change, will we be ashamed and embarrassed later about our past? What will happen when *who I am now* becomes *who I used to be*?

I was there. I remember.

But God says, *There's grace for imperfection. I have a pardon all ready for you.*

To the one fighting shame and fear and control – and those are the same things, really – He says, *I know you're not perfect. I know you need growth. I know your past, your upbringing, and the indignities you've suffered and in-flicted.* And He still wants you closer. No shame, no fear, no stumbling.

Most of us can run from our past, but it takes strength to face it, sift through the rubble, and let God wash through it.

The enemy wants us to be cowards – weak and easily manipulated. Any wretch can deny, lie, or persist in wrong thinking or wrong behavior. It takes guts to turn your face toward light when you've been hiding in shadows. It takes a special kind of bravery to admit fault, be teachable, and turn.

It takes grit and valor to start over.

Ephesians 2:1-6 says:

> *And you were dead in the trespasses and sins in which you once walked [used to, but not anymore], following the course of this world, following the prince of the power of the air, the spirit that is now at work in the sons of disobedience — among whom we all once lived in the passions of our flesh [past tense], carrying out the desires of the body and the mind, and were [not "are"] by nature children of wrath, like the rest of mankind. But God —*

(I love this part. Ready?)

But God, being rich in mercy, because of the great love with which he loved us, even when we were dead in our trespasses, made us alive together with Christ — by grace you have been saved — and raised us up with him and seated us with him in the heavenly places in Christ Jesus.

God made a way for shame to leave, for you to live free. Shame off you, shame off me.

We are the washed ones – covered by Him, and at the same time, set free.

questions to consider:

- What automatic responses do you have that reflect pride or insecurity? Or shame, control, or fear?
- If you ask God to tell you who you are, what does He say?
- What might your future look like if you take a hard area from your past and allow the Lord to wash through it?

(more) scripture for today:

I do not cease to give thanks for you, remembering you in my prayers, that the God of our Lord Jesus Christ, the Father of glory, may give you the Spirit of wisdom and of revelation in the knowledge of him, having the eyes of your hearts enlightened, that you may know what is the hope to which he has called you, what are the riches of his glorious inheritance in the saints.

- Ephesians 1:16-18

_____

_____

_____

_____

_____

_____

_____

DAY 7

THRESHOLD

God has questions for us. Are you ready?

He asks us things like, *If it didn't matter what anyone else thought...And if it didn't matter who noticed...And if it didn't matter who paid attention...**What would you let Me do in your life?***

This concept of **threshold** meets us where we're at and then challenges us to see our future from God's perspective. It's the link between our dreams and the obedience required to get there.

He asks us, *How would you let Me move? Where would you let Me take you? Can I carry you over the threshold?*

I can come up with all kinds of crazy ideas, but for them to be more than just words on paper I have to give God permission to move in me, through me, around me. And when I think of what that means, it's a little Be Careful What You Ask For-ish.

So many times, I've thought I met my threshold for change, growth, and painful stretching. But God said, *This is a different kind of threshold. The kind that is a doorway. This kind of threshold means Beginning, Birth, Dawn, Entrance.*
It requires obedience, surrender, and God's perspective to cross it.

As we continue to pray relentless-style – right as we're doing the dishes, changing diapers, driving to work, encouraging a friend, and telling the phone solicitor for the umpteenth time, *No, I don't have ten minutes to answer just a few questions* – we are storming castles. Right then, as we are praying, abiding, recognizing His presence in every moment, the captives are being set free.

But this doesn't mean that praying without ceasing is a "stay in your comfort zone free" card. Praying does not let us off the hook in serving others, getting involved, giving extravagantly, or anything else that gets our hands dirty. Our mission is firmly outside the comfort zone.

What unceasing prayer will do is give us greater wisdom for how He wants us to accomplish those things, which eliminates much of the anxiety and discomfort that doing them might cause otherwise.

And this is important, because He will ask us to do things that feel bigger than we are.

This habit of relentless prayer broadens the limits that we set for ourselves. Little steps become big steps. Those big steps get easier and start to feel like little steps. And before you know it, your comfort zone has grown deep and wide and you're still pushing the edges of it outward:

You, pursuing that thing He's called you to.

Me, pursuing that thing He called me to.

Fearless, relentless, while we pray for our country and its messes, and our families and their futures, and the active clean-up operation in our own hearts – and suddenly, that castle is ours.

questions to consider:

- If it didn't matter what anyone else thought, what would you let God do in your life?
- What dreams do you have that feel too big for you?
- When you ask God about them, what specific thing is He telling you to do next?

scripture for today:

> *For, "Yet a little while, and the coming one will come and will not delay; but my righteous one shall live by faith, and if he shrinks back, my soul has no pleasure in him." But we are not of those who shrink back and are destroyed, but of those who have faith and preserve their souls.*
>
> *- Hebrews 10:37-39*

> *And without faith it is impossible to please him, for whoever would draw near to God must believe that he exists and that he rewards those who seek him.*
>
> *- Hebrews 11:6*

_____

_____

_____

_____

_____

_____

DAY 8

THRESHOLD

This probably never happens to you, but every once in a while in the middle of the night when I'm supposed to be sleeping, a list of concerns starts parading through my thoughts: Bad habits cropping up in some of our children. Appointments I keep forgetting to make. Something I said during the day that I'm just positive someone misunderstood or took the wrong way...and I'm seriously fretting, overwhelmed, and feeding the beast.

I can't cross the threshold because I'm so busy filling my mind with all worries and problems I have on this side of the doorway. I know I'm supposed to pray but instead I backslide into the opposite.

And when I'm exhausted in the middle of the night, my to-do list looks so magnified that I feel done in before the day has even had a chance to start. How am I gonna cross the threshold, when I can barely get out of bed?

But God is right there with me. He says, *Hey, Love. Your night vision is inflating your problems. Try a different point of view: Magnify Me instead. Picture the victory.*

It's hard at first. I try to imagine one of our kids who had early childhood trauma being healed and free. Sometimes that feels so far off, so impossible, that it takes me a while to even think of what that would look like. But after a few minutes of asking God for His perspective on it, I get it – and then in less than two seconds it becomes prayer.

It's the breakthrough we're praying toward.

It's not just me asking God for healing, although that's a good start. It's me asking God for what the fullness of that healing looks like – I'm asking God to show me His perspective on this situation. What does it look like beyond that threshold?

Over and over, with every issue He reminds me:

Picture the victory.

My list is long, but He's not tired and I'm not going anywhere. He's right there, ready to tackle the big stuff with me. So I picture assignments done quickly. I picture health issues, gone. I picture a kid who deals with extreme anxiety going about his day in peace.

This isn't some new age idea. It's scripture, obeyed.

Mark 11:24 says:

*Therefore I tell you, whatever you ask in prayer, believe that
you have received it, and it will be yours.*

And Matthew 21:21-22 says:

*And Jesus answered them, "Truly, I say to you, if you have faith
and do not doubt, you will not only do what has been done to the
fig tree, but even if you say to this mountain, 'Be taken up and
thrown into the sea,' it will happen. And whatever you ask in
prayer, you will receive, if you have faith."*

I picture the victory of special needs healed, casting those mountains to the sea,
because He can. Because He wants to teach me how, and He wants me to remember to do it instead of feeding my own anxiety and letting it wreak havoc in the
middle of the night, or during the day.

The day ahead becomes do-able. Fretting and fears diminished. Faith and
hope rising. It's more than just my feelings – the future changes when we pray this
way. We are the clean-up operation, working the night shift.

> *Ye fearful saints, fresh courage take*
> *The clouds ye so much dread*
> *Are big with mercy, and shall break*
> *In blessings on your head.*
> *His purposes will ripen fast,*
> *Unfolding every hour;*
> *The bud may have a bitter taste*
> *But sweet will be the flower.*
> *- William Cowper*

questions to consider:

- What are three things that you need answers or resolution for in this
  season?
- Ask God: What might the victory look like in each of those situations?
- What do those victories tell you about God's character? And what do they
  tell you about your own identity?

(more) scripture for today:

That is why it depends on faith, in order that the promise may rest on grace and be guaranteed to all his offspring—not only to the adherent of the law but also to the one who shares the faith of Abraham, who is the father of us all, as it is written, "I have made you the father of many nations"—in the presence of the God in whom he believed, who gives life to the dead and calls into existence the things that do not exist.

- Romans 4:16-17

_____

_____

_____

_____

_____

_____

_____

_____

_____

_____

_____

_____

_____

_____

_____

_____

_____

_____

DAY 9

THRESHOLD

Sometimes God asks us to do something that seems like it's not "you." What if His prompting feels too intimidating, too unfamiliar, too hard, too new?

It might be that He's talking to us about a Big Thing. That thing we can't stop thinking about but feels out of reach, or that Next Big Thing that we keep pushing to the back of our minds because we have no idea how to begin it. And we're nervous about talking to someone about it or even praying about it because, well, when you do that, things might get a little more serious... and we're not so sure we want it to be serious.

And He tells us, *Oh, Love...who do you think you are, anyway? Don't you really want to know who you are? Because you're so much more than who you limit yourself to be inside the safety of your comfort zone.*

Sometimes when we say we are waiting on God to cross a threshold, the truth is we're just not trusting Him. We settle for so little in the stalling to obey. How do we tell the difference? How can we tell if we're stalling, or if we're actually waiting on God?

God will often ask us this question:

Did you do what I already told you?

And often my answer is, *Well, yes. I mean, sort of. Mostly, I think.*

I sound a lot like my sons when I ask them if they made their beds in the morning. Almost always, the truth is...no.

"No, not really," they answer. "I didn't really do it all the way, I just sorta spread the top blanket around to cover up the wrinkly sheets underneath. I thought that would be good enough."

God tells me the same thing I tell them: *Go back and check again. Dig a little deeper, more than just making things look good on the surface. Do it right once, and you won't have to ask Me if it's done, because you'll know it is.*

When we are stalling, looking for a sign, sometimes what we're really asking is, *Is it good enough?*

So how do we know if we're stalling, or waiting? When we are truly waiting on Him, we're all-in and have obeyed in taking that step outside the comfort zone. We won't be looking for a back-up plan, because we didn't bring one.

It means we are invested, and ready to move forward.

Because **forward** is where obedience takes us.

questions to consider:

- How are you different inside your comfort zone versus outside of your comfort zone?
- Do you tend to think too small about yourself, your callings, and your dreams? What does it look like to think of these things with God's perspective instead of your own?
- Are you stalling in anything God has told you to do? What is your next step?

scripture for today:

And when the soles of the feet of the priests bearing the ark of the Lord, the Lord of all the earth, shall rest in the waters of the Jordan [when you go forward in obedience], the waters of the Jordan shall be cut off from flowing, and the waters coming down from above shall stand in one heap.

- Joshua 3:13

He said, "But I will be with you, and this shall be the sign for you, that I have sent you: when you have brought the people out of Egypt [obeyed in doing what I already told you to do], you shall serve God on this mountain."

- Exodus 3:12

_____

_____

_____

_____

_____

_____

_____

_____

_____

DAY 10

FORWARD

Throughout my adulthood I've heard women rave about this one thing, claiming it changed their lives forever.

It's not essential oils. Not the latest self-help book. Not even Jesus. I'm talking about The Amazing, The Miraculous, The Inexplicably Marvelous Phenomenon known as...a crock pot.

I was just never interested in owning one. But people told me "Just throw your ingredients in, and dinner magically appears several hours later!" so eventually I decided that, maybe, I could use some of that magic in my life.

I chopped. I tossed in ingredients. I put the lid on. And thought, *This is going to be awesome*...Except it wasn't. Two hours later, I realized it probably does work perfectly, unless you forget to plug it in. That part is really, super important.

Let's go back to talking about the threshold: Not everyone wants us to walk through it. There's greatness beyond and an enemy who doesn't want us to go there. So we cross the threshold and arrows fly at us – words from others, words in our heads, situations that seem impossible. Forward growth is messy.

But God tells us, *You have what you need to walk through safely. You just have to remember how to operate it.* Crockpots do nothing when they're turned off; neither does our faith when we waver.

Ephesians 6:16 says:

> *In all circumstances take up the shield of faith, with which you can extinguish all the flaming darts of the evil one.*

God reminds us, *I've given you a picture of the victory. Hold it high.* That faith – the vision He gives us, picturing the victory He has ahead – is our shield. It covers and protects our families and our marriages. And it is really, super important.

Hold it high, He says. *And don't hesitate when I tell you to move.*

Moving forward puts us on unfamiliar ground, out of our comfort zone, out of our control. So sometimes we take what we can't control – even if it's something we've longed for – and we sabotage it. We are a bird in a cage with the gate wide open, dreaming about flight but continuously shutting the door on ourselves.

We think that if we fail, it's on us. If it doesn't work out, crushing disappointment mocks us. We can't control what happens because we've never been here before. It's easier to avoid it all in the first place.

Will we take the risk? Or will we make excuses? Put it off? Push it aside, and try to convince ourselves we're doing so for responsible reasons?

Obedience often looks less like something we do and more like something we believe. And obedience starts in our minds and in our thoughts. We are obeying God when we trust Him.

We obey God when we choose hope over everything else – our excuses, our anxieties, and our fears.

Hope is a powerful fuel, and when combined with the truth of God's goodness and trustworthiness, it turns fear, doubt, despair, and discouragement to ashes. Our prayer is a bellows, breathing oxygen everywhere the fire needs to be kindled.

questions to consider:

- Where are you having difficulty moving forward? What specific fears, anxieties, concerns, or circumstances are in your way?
- Ask God about each of these. What truths can you counter each of them with?
- What does faith look like in each of those situations?

(more) scripture for today:

What then shall we say to these things? If God is for us, who can be against us? He who did not spare his own Son but gave him up for us all, how will he not also with him graciously give us all things?

- Romans 8:31-32

No, in all these things we are more than conquerors through him who loved us.

- Romans 8:37

_____

_____

_____

_____

DAY 11

FORWARD

Almost every time I move forward, I get this sinking, dropping feeling right under my ribs, a volley of fiery arrows the enemy uses every time I'm at the threshold of anything. Sometimes I fight it for days in a row, first thing in the morning, right out of the gate.

It's called fear, and fear wants to be entertained. Fear is an attention-seeker, a bully, an insecure narcissist with no vision of its own. Instead, fear steals your vision, warps and counterfeits it, and hands it back to you posing as the real deal – only, by that time, it's ugly and twisted.

We cannot use our imagination to create a picture of all the possible evils that might occur in any given situation. It's not just worrying; it's a temptation we must resist because our very lives are at stake.

Fear and worry are not the same thing as wise preparation and they will never ensure safety. In fact, they can actually grant permission to the opposite while giving us a false sense of security because we think we've thought of all the terrible potential scenarios to our situation. It is a counterfeit that we must not fall for.

Fear knocks on our door in disguise as a security technician, when in fact he is an unrepentant criminal trespassing on our property – someone we don't want anywhere near our children. If you so much as invite fear in for tea, it will move in, take over, and rearrange your furniture. Fear is a lousy houseguest.

Do not ask for fear's opinion on things. It is a presumptuous narcissist that takes your keys and invites its friends over. And doubt, despair, and discouragement? You don't like fear's friends. You don't want them in your house at all.

Jesus tells us in Matthew 11:29-30:

> *Take My yoke upon you, and learn from Me, for I am gentle and lowly in heart, and you will find rest for your souls. For My yoke is easy, and My burden is light.*

The burden we carry – the light yoke – is to refuse to carry the heavy burden fear tries to place on us. The light yoke is obedience – because the consequences of giving into fear are way more than we want to carry.

God calls us to surrender, moving forward in obedience, not shrinking back. Fear and control will court us away from victory. But surrendered obedience is rest, joy, and power.

I remember the story of the old man who said on his deathbed that he had had a lot of trouble in his life, most of which had never happened.

- Winston Churchill

questions to consider:

- What are some true statements you can arm yourself with as you move forward?
- How can you use your imagination to fight fear instead of giving in to it?
- What does surrendered obedience look like for you today?

(more) scripture for today:

Through [Jesus] we have also obtained access by faith into this grace in which we stand, and we rejoice in hope of the glory of God.

- Romans 5:2

Finally, brothers, whatever is true, whatever is honorable, whatever is just, whatever is pure, whatever is lovely, whatever is commendable, if there is any excellence, if there is anything worthy of praise, think about these things.

- Philippians 4:8

_____

_____

_____

_____

_____

_____

_____

_____

DAY 12

FORWARD

Do events turn out differently when we allow fear to creep in? Yeah. They do. You know that Jesus wasn't the only one to walk on water, right? Peter did, too. Here's Matthew 14:25-29:

> And in the fourth watch of the night he came to them, walking on the sea. But when the disciples saw him walking on the sea, they were terrified, and said, "It is a ghost!" and they cried out in fear. But immediately Jesus spoke to them, saying, "Take heart; it is I. Do not be afraid."
>
> And Peter answered him, "Lord, if it is you, command me to come to you on the water." He said, "Come." So Peter got out of the boat and walked on the water and came to Jesus.

And then you know what happens. Or...maybe you don't. I always thought Peter saw the waves, started to sink, freaked out, and was hauled up by Jesus. But that's not what happened.

Matthew 14:30-31:

> But when he saw the wind, he was afraid, and beginning to sink he cried out, "Lord, save me." Jesus immediately reached out his hand and took hold of him, saying to him, "O you of little faith, why did you doubt?"

Peter saw the wind, and then he was afraid. And then he started to sink. He wasn't sinking before. His fear induced the sinking. It was, literally, that sinking, dropping feeling.

We can't hold high the shield of faith while entertaining fear at the same time. It's only one or the other, and both will cause something to happen. We have to choose. The end of the story will be different depending on that choice. When we entertain fear, we align with it. When we entertain faith, we align with faith.

Situations with our kids, our families, our country – we have high hopes, we pray hard, but doubt, despair, fear, and discouragement sell us some sob-story version of our hopes and dreams.

They obscure our vision of reality. They want us to see the job loss, but not the opportunity right around the corner. They want to show off the conflict, but not

54

the deeper wisdom that results from it. They want to illuminate the wrinkles, but make you forget about the character and experience that came with those lines. Doubt, despair, fear, and discouragement never give us the full story.

We are to abide with God, and when we do so, His perfect love casts out fear. But here's the danger: If we're not abiding and aligning with God, we naturally swing the other way and abide with fear. **Do not fear** is a command, not a suggestion, for good reason. Fear doesn't care for permission; it just wants access. The counterfeit picture of what we're afraid of may be the key that permits that access.

But agreeing with God, picturing the victory and trusting Him for what He has promised, strips the enemy of power he would take from us otherwise. Trusting God is the fatal, final blow that puts fear out of our misery.

questions to consider:

- What does entertaining faith look like in the area you're moving forward in?
- How does God's perfect love cast out your fear?
- What does trusting God and abiding with Him look like for you today?

(more) scripture for today:

> The sting of death is sin, and the power of sin is the law. But thanks be to God, who gives us the victory through our Lord Jesus Christ. Therefore, my beloved brothers, be steadfast, immovable, always abounding in the work of the Lord, knowing that in the Lord your labor is not in vain.
>
> - 1 Corinthians 15:56-58

> For God gave us a spirit not of fear but of power and love and self-control.
>
> - 2 Timothy 1:7

_____

_____

_____

_____

_____

DAY 13

FRIENDSHIP

Several years ago our family joined a bulk food co-op. This meant that instead of shopping at the grocery store like normal people, where we would get normal sizes of things like oatmeal, cornmeal, and raisins – which, in our family, only last about fourteen minutes– now we buy most of our dry goods through this co-op. We get huuuge bags that last for months. A bag of oatmeal could double as a toddler mattress.

We should have joined years earlier; I'm not sure why it took us so long. After a while, we'd heard so many endorsements from friends that we couldn't ignore it anymore. I don't usually think of myself as a follower but when a trusted friend tells me where to go to buy tea and gourmet popcorn at a fraction of the store price, I'm happy to let them lead me.

Which brings us back to thresholds, and moving forward, leading others into obedience, and the Jordan River.

Joshua and the rest of the Israelites are getting ready to cross the Jordan River. Here are their instructions in Joshua 3:2-3:

> At the end of three days the officers went through the camp and commanded the people, "As soon as you see the ark of the covenant of the Lord your God being carried by the Levitical priests, then you shall set out from your place and follow it."

The priests needed to obey before the people followed.

Sometimes our obedience and boldness is the sign God has placed for someone else to see. At such a time as this, our willingness may be what they are watching for. Our obedience can be the best kind of contagious, creating a culture that moves forward.

Friendship rooted in prayer, challenging us to obedience, is a powerful force to be reckoned with. The enemy takes notice and shrinks back.

Here's what happened in the enemy camp when God's people moved forward in obedience together:

Joshua 5:1:

As soon as all the kings of the Amorites who were beyond the Jordan to the west, and all the kings of the Canaanites who were by the sea, heard that the Lord had dried up the waters of the Jordan for the people of Israel until they had crossed over, their hearts melted and there was no longer any spirit in them because of the people of Israel.

We need each other. A united front creates a force to be reckoned with.

We need to pray with and for each other as much as possible, prayer that goes deep and wide and maybe even unnoticed by the one we pray for.

So much is at stake in these small acts.

They are often the covering that keeps someone from giving up before the victory comes.

questions to consider:

- How has God used you to lead friends forward? How has God used certain friends to lead you forward?
- Who can you pray for today that needs a boost toward victory?
- What might God be calling you to step into that will spur others toward obedience, also?

(more) scripture for today:

Five of you shall chase a hundred, and a hundred of you shall chase ten thousand, and your enemies shall fall before you by the sword.

- Leviticus 26:8

_____

_____

_____

_____

_____

_____

_____

_____

DAY 14

FRIENDSHIP

Here's a verse you're probably familiar with. Ready?
John 15:5:

> *I am the vine; you are the branches. Whoever abides in me and I
> in him, he it is that bears much fruit, for apart from me you can
> do nothing.*

We know this verse so well it threatens to numb us in familiarity. We know that we bear fruit when we abide in God's presence. We pay so much attention to this that sometimes we overlook the other role of branches that are connected to the vine: they are a covering for those who seek refuge.

We run to Jesus, the Vine, so we can be His hands and feet to others when they come to us. Branches are a shelter and the vulnerable run to them for protection. They provide safety for small creatures seeking sanctuary from predators. It's where they build nests; it's where they give birth to new life, and it's where they raise their families.

We are that for others, they are that for us. Friends, family, church, and home are the emotional shelters we cultivate for each other — these are the relationships where we nurse our wounds and rest after a hard day. They're the school that teaches and grows us, and sometimes, they're our emergency room. It is where life is protected.

God told me, *I've called you to increase courage in each other because you will need it. If you are not speaking life and victory over each other, you are in retreat.*

In my marriage and my friendships, God often reminds me that we need to show grace to each other and trust that He is speaking to each of us instead of getting offended over slight disagreements and misunderstandings. Our effectiveness diminishes in proportion to our friendly fire.

Because when we are united, our impact is exponential. This is where we find the victory.

Galatians 6:9-10 says:

And let us not grow weary of doing good, for in due season we
will reap, if we do not give up. So then, as we have opportunity,
let us do good to everyone, and especially to those who are of the
household of faith.

These friends are the ones we go to battle with. They're also the ones we go to battle for.

We save each other every day by living in deep and wide community and connection, preventing isolation and retreat.

We are meant to advance, but we go farthest together.

questions to consider:

- Who has provided spiritual shelter for you lately? How can you pray for them today?
- What have your friends done to increase courage in you?
- How can you increase courage in your friends in this season?

(more) scripture for today:

Beloved, let us love one another, for love is from God,
and whoever loves has been born of God and knows God.

- 1 John 4:7

One man of you puts to flight a thousand, since it is the
Lord your God who fights for you, just as he promised you.

- Joshua 23:10

_____

_____

_____

_____

_____

_____

_____

DAY 15

FRIENDSHIP

Several years ago our family was going through a really hard, dark period that lasted a couple of years. And within those two years, two of the families who we were closest to moved thousands of miles away. It was the worst time (for us) for it to happen.

It takes a while for "new people" to become "our people" but we have them now. These are the ones we spill our thoughts, feelings, and ideas to with confidence. They bring balance to my overthinking, salt my perspective with their own wisdom, and keep me out of trouble (which means they make me practice social skills).

Together we've dealt with kids who were out of control, crises in the middle of the night, and medical emergencies. We've met in the courthouse, and the hospital, we've celebrated and grieved together. And we've grown deeper roots the more we've covered each other.

Sometimes we get lost in the wilderness. And God is our refuge, of course — but in His abundant generosity, He also gives us friends to confirm His wisdom and to comfort us as we navigate the dark forest.

Psalm 31:19-20 says:

Oh, how abundant is your goodness, which you have stored up for those who fear you and worked for those who take refuge in you, in the sight of the children of mankind! In the cover of your presence you hide them from the plots of men; you store them in your shelter from the strife of tongues.

For over two years I went through a dark season, plowing through expectations, obligations, the feeling of never doing enough, never being enough, and not having the time or emotional margin to do more than walk around in circles. I knew that grace was there, but I couldn't see it; I knew that I was supposed to feel free, but instead I felt fried. But my friends could see it for me. Those closest to me spoke freedom into me when I didn't have the words for myself.

We need each other's point of view so we can have each other's back. Through our prayers, our friendship, and our words, we shield those around us from harm. We comfort them when they're hurting and create a safe place to rest and grow as they seek Him. Our friendships are the haven, the hospice, and occasionally the theater that provides comic relief after a hard day. God made us to be a covering for each other.

We don't stay there constantly. There's a whole forest to be tended, loved, and known as we reach out to provide the comfort He gives us to the communities around us.

Sometimes we're the temporary hostel for acquaintances and strangers just passing through. We are His hands and feet when we comfort our crying child, our hurting friend, and the weeping stranger. As we pray and move, He calls us to be the rescue mission, the special ops team, the trauma center that reaches out to others who seek His sanctuary.

But we do come back to our own nest in the bracken — these close relationships that nurture us — to rest, reassess, and recuperate.

These relationships are the cocoon in our daily lives and in crisis. We hide there in His protection as we walk with each other through metamorphosis and change, from death to life. We are meant to fly together.

> *There is nothing I would not do for those who are really my friends. I have no notion of loving people by halves, it is not my nature.*
>
> *- Jane Austen* [3]

questions to consider:

- How have certain friendships helped you obey in God's calling for your life?
- What was a time in your life when friendship made the difference between victory and defeat?
- Who are you flying with in this season? How can you pray for them today?

(more) scripture for today:

> *Blessed be the God and Father of our Lord Jesus Christ, the Father of mercies and God of all comfort, who comforts us in all our affliction, so that we may be able to comfort those who are in any affliction, with the comfort with which we ourselves are comforted by God.*
>
> *- 2 Corinthians 1:3-4*

DAY 16

FIRE

I love books. I'm not a great reader, though – not a fast reader – just a scattered, slow reader. So it took me two and a half years, but I finally finished reading *Les Miserables*. And in it, I read about a major cleanup operation: the saturated underground sewer system in Paris.

It really did happen, and in the book it starts like this:

> "It was a formidable campaign; a nocturnal battle against pestilence and suffocation."

It's safe, nothing graphic. Let's keep going.

> "The operation was complicated; the visit entailed the necessity of cleaning; hence it was necessary to cleanse and at the same time, to proceed...They advanced with toil. The lanterns pined away in the foul atmosphere. From time to time, a fainting sewerman was carried out."

The project was tackled in 1805 because one man was willing to go into the putrid darkness and do something about it.

His name was Pierre Bruneseau. He did what needed to be done in the place and time he lived in, willing to be the cleanup operation and go into the dark when others shuddered at the thought of it.

God nudged me as I read about it. What would happen if each of us took this approach with prayer? What would happen if those darkest, most hopeless places, institutions, and people were tackled in prayer on a level that no one has had the grit and persistence to take on before?

What if we prayed – really prayed, with bright, life-giving detail? What if we were brave enough to picture what it would look like if the darkest businesses were replaced with ones that breathed life in a community – and then we prayed it into existence?

Because God teaches us to pray in ways that simultaneously prevent events from happening and also in ways that create things into being. We learn the relentless, without-ceasing part: During a sermon, we're interceding for the pastor and the people as we listen; during conversation, we're changing a one-on-one discussion into a conference call with God, whether the other person knows it or not; during our reading and study, we talk to God about the words on the page and discern whether or not they align with truth.

John 1:5 says:

> *The light shines in the darkness, and the darkness has not*
> *overcome it.*

Throughout the day we're praying, and not just in the quiet available moments. During laundry, during the commute, during the phone call with the specialist, *so help me* – we're asking, *Lord, what are Your words here?*

And He's right there, waking us up to bring light into dark places.

questions to consider:

- What dark place is God calling you to tackle in prayer? What would victory look like in that area?
- What times of the day are the easiest for you to hear God and pray? Why is that?
- What might praying without ceasing look like in the other normal routines of your day?

(more) scripture for today:

> *For we do not wrestle against flesh and blood, but against the*
> *rulers, against the authorities, against the cosmic powers over*
> *this present darkness, against the spiritual forces of evil in the*
> *heavenly places. Therefore take up the whole armor of God, that*
> *you may be able to withstand in the evil day, and having done*
> *all, to stand firm.*
>
> *- Ephesians 6:12-13*

_____

_____

_____

_____

_____

_____

_____

DAY 17

FIRE

A friend said this in a sermon once and it stuck with me: *The presence of fire in the Bible often symbolizes the presence of God.* The fire on the mountain, the burning bush, the pillar of smoke, the tongues of fire. God's presence sanctifies, purifies, covers, and brings light.

Hebrews 12:28-29 says:

> *Therefore let us be grateful for receiving a kingdom that cannot be shaken, and thus let us offer to God acceptable worship, with reverence and awe, for our God is a consuming fire.*

When we pray for the lost, the light yoke of surrender is only a breath away. The heavy yoke of filth and blackness costs so much, and it lies to those who are in it that the effort to take the deep breath of surrender isn't worth it. But what if we made the road smoother for them through prayer that refuses to give up?

I've also been the one who was lost, and losing, and needed someone to fight in prayer for me. Many of us would not be who we are today without those who fought the darkness for us.

We have loved ones stuck in this kind of mire, and this is where the fight comes in for those of us who love them and are tempted to just wash our hands and give up on them. Giving up seems easier to us, just as it seems to them, because the pain of disappointment after raising our hopes is so hard to bear.

But this stubborn, unyielding prayer is where we fight, because the decision between hope and despair is where the battle rages. This is where the outcome of victory or defeat is decided. We can be the powerful loving ones, clinging to a healthy vision of the one who is lost in darkness, refusing to let it go. We can also refuse to let go.

1 Peter 5:8-9 says:

> *Be sober-minded; be watchful. Your adversary the devil prowls around like a roaring lion, seeking someone to devour. Resist him, firm in your faith, knowing that the same kinds of suffering are being experienced by your brotherhood throughout the world.*

74

We cling to this hope and pray it into existence regardless of the blackness that pulses and threatens. We could fade away and give up, but heroes run into the battle and not away from it. Our loved ones need us to be those heroes – because they too are meant to be heroes, and that's why the enemy fights so desperately for them.

That enemy whispers, "Give up. Lower your weapons."

And we respond: "Fire."

questions to consider:

- Who needs you to fight for them in prayer in this season? What breakthrough do they need?
- Do you struggle with feeling hopeless or jaded about a particular situation or person? If so, what does God say about it?
- What would a "beyond your wildest dreams" victory look like for that situation or person?

(more) scripture for today:

...praying at all times in the Spirit, with all prayer and supplication. To that end, keep alert with all perseverance, making supplication for all the saints, and also for me, that words may be given to me in opening my mouth boldly to proclaim the mystery of the gospel, for which I am an ambassador in chains, that I may declare it boldly, as I ought to speak.

- Ephesians 6:18-20

_____

_____

_____

_____

_____

_____

_____

DAY 18

FIRE

Confession time, housewife edition: I don't do spring cleaning, I don't rearrange furniture for fun, and I don't overhaul closets in the fall. Those are deceptive, sneaky projects.

In the attempt to take them on you make a bigger mess than you had in the first place, and there's no end to it. You tackle one simple thing, like de-cluttering a few kitchen cabinets, and suddenly you're surrounded by gadgets to donate to the thrift store, unidentifiable spices that lost their aroma sometime before Y2K, and a depression-era bottle of corn syrup permanently cemented to the back of the shelf.

If it was just cleaning – or phone calls, or errands – it wouldn't be so daunting. But those tasks compound with bigger, more complicated things, that don't fit neatly on a to-do list: Hard relationships. Hard decisions. Health issues, deadlines, changes, and clutter. Those things that float around, making mental noise and disorder. They're not even all bad; mostly, they're just taking up far more space than any one situation rightfully should, like a two-year-old with a mocha. And it's not that the concerns aren't real or don't need to be addressed. But stacked on top of each other, they magnify way out of proportion from stress, exhaustion, and fear.

Instead of grasping at all these issues out of my reach, God is teaching me to bring them down to earth where I can put them under authority and see them for what they are.

Psalm 112:7-8 says:

> *He is not afraid of bad news; his heart is firm, trusting in the Lord. His heart is steady; he will not be afraid, until he looks in triumph on his adversaries.*

Sometimes these situations seem like adversaries. Whatever they are, I'm learning to nail them down. I just use my old journal, but I don't think you don't have to be a writer to do this.

The stress, sickness, chaos, and deadlines get filtered onto the paper, one thing at a time. As I write each thing down, big and small, they're caught and pinned. They might squirm a little but they're not going anywhere, and I can look them in the eye and rest again. And when I read it later, all of those things are brought down to the right size.

It's completely honest, nothing fancy – it's rough, unrefined, kind of like the tree that Jesus nailed everything to 2000 years ago.

It is us, hushed, listening for Him.

It is praying on paper. He speaks when we listen, and for me, the clutter is quieter and He is louder when I write it out. All those issues come down a peg, brought down to size before the One who really knows what to do about all of it.

It's significant that paper is made from the same material He was nailed to. He still uses it to heal us, show us more of Him, and conquer what's harassing us.

And it's important to conquer what's harassing us, because it is hard to pray for others when we're consumed with our own stuff. But when we deal with that stuff, we can pursue prayer and intercession for others, and God teaches us to notice things we never would have on our own.

We look out the window and instead of just staring at the leaves whipping across the street, we intercede for the neighbor who lives there. We pray for her house, her safety, her warmth through the winter. We pray for the neighbors to be kind, patient, and gracious to each other. We pray for a sense of community, respect, and camaraderie. And there goes the neighborhood.

We get to help make the headlines of history, and lights are turning on everywhere.

questions to consider:

- What does intercession look like for you, outside the box?
- How has God taught you to handle overwhelm?
- What specific historical headlines would you like your prayers to influence?

(more) scripture for today:

Therefore take up the whole armor of God, that you may be able to withstand in the evil day, and having done all, to stand firm. Stand therefore, having fastened on the belt of truth, and having put on the breastplate of righteousness, and, as shoes for your feet, having put on the readiness given by the gospel of peace.

- Ephesians 6:13-15

_____

_____

_____

_____

DAY 19

LIGHT

One morning recently I came downstairs, got my coffee, and my first interaction with one kid was to be informed of an impossible math problem she was working on - no "good morning," no hug or kiss, no nothing.

The math problem, my daughter informed me, involved "some stupid character" buying a "stupid toy" for her "stupid little dog" and something about "stupid taxes" and subtracting numbers that could not be subtracted and "*UGH MATH BLAGGHH THISISIMPOSSIBLE!*"

I looked at the problem and informed her that the numbers were supposed to be added, not subtracted.

"Huh. Thanks," she said, and went back to her room. Still no hug or anything. But at least she was up early doing her schoolwork, right?

If you've ever spent time with kids, you know that correcting, teaching, and answering their questions all day long can be exhausting. Every conversation we engage in – whether it's with our kids, our coworkers, our neighbors, whoever – changes or maintains the atmosphere of our home, office, ministry, and community, for better or worse. Our words and tone keep us close to each other or they push us apart. Our conversations can leave others full or empty.

Colossians 4:6 says:

> *Let your speech always be gracious, seasoned with salt, so that*
> *you may know how you ought to answer each person.*

Life is messy, full of tough situations and emotional topics and impossible problems that require heaps of wisdom and self-control in order to keep our conversations filled with grace. We have conversations with our kids about things like reproduction. Or divorce. Or...arithmetic. You know it's true.

Our relentless prayer is behind the scenes, life-transforming, future-changing, people-saving work, but it's not glittering and sophisticated. It's rugged, rustic, primitive – beautiful in humility, sincerity, and imperfection. It is the movement underground that builds until the earth shakes.

It's not just requests and intercession. It's not just praise and thankfulness. Mostly, it's His presence encompassing every type of prayer, like music that permeates every room of a house.

That daughter I mentioned earlier was four years old when she asked how she could give her heart to Jesus. I told her, "You tell Him you want to follow Him ...that means you let Him be your boss."

She was incredulous. "He's gonna *boss* me?!"

"He's the nicest boss," I told her. "If you don't know what to do, you can ask Him and He'll help you do the right thing. And...you know what? When you obey Him, I don't have to boss you so much." What a deal.

She asked, "Can I hear Him boss me?"

"Yep," I answered. "You usually hear Him inside you. His voice is gentle. You recognize it with practice."

She ran off to play while I was still thinking of the words that just came out of my mouth. He uses these kids to teach us so much.

God asked me, *Did you hear that? My voice is gentle. You learned to recognize it with practice. And you learn to imitate My voice with practice, too.*

It doesn't matter if we go from the kitchen to the office, or from interceding to just waiting to hear His voice – the Music is there, filling every room of the house.

questions to consider:

- When have your words or tone (or someone else's words or tone) made all the difference in a situation?
- Where do you see words making a Kingdom impact on your culture?
- How do you find yourself imitating God's voice?

(more) scripture for today:

Love one another with brotherly affection.

Outdo one another in showing honor.

Do not be slothful in zeal, be fervent in spirit, serve the Lord.

Rejoice in hope, be patient in tribulation, be constant in prayer.

Contribute to the needs of the saints and seek to show hospitality.

- Romans 12:10-13

DAY 20

LIGHT

In the "Fire" section of this study, I told you that I don't do spring cleaning. But I *do* clean on a normal basis. And I'm learning to pray that God would be cleaning me, and us, as I clean the house.

As I'm scrubbing grime around the sink faucets, I'm asking Him to remove hardened areas and stubbornness. When I'm dusting neglected areas, I'm asking Him to reveal things that need attention and care. Folding towels, I'm thanking Him for clean water and healthy bodies, and praying for those who have neither. While sorting the kids' laundry, I'm praying that they would be grateful for what they have, steward their things well, and not be immature whiners. And I'm praying that for me, too.

Colossians 3:23-24 says:

> *Whatever you do, work heartily, as for the Lord and not for men, knowing that from the Lord you will receive the inheritance as your reward. You are serving the Lord Christ.*

Some seasons in life are hard, or confusing, or painfully dry, and God meets us where we are. Some nights, I am exhausted, and bedtime can't come soon enough. We barely skid to 8 pm, and I don't feel warm, gentle, or full of grace.

Our three oldest boys used to share a bedroom. I would shut their door and collapse on the couch, depleted, and suddenly hear all sorts of whooping and revelry above me, where they were acting out some wild rumpus and I had to break up the party.

I'd love to tell you how it went: I sigh and walk up the stairs. I open their door, and calmly – *calmly*, I tell you – remind them to be quiet. "This is Mama's rest time, Sweeties, and you need to be in bed, reading or sleeping." And, of course, they obey like perfect little lambs, with no baaaahing for the rest of the night.

It would be so awesome to tell you that. But I would be lying.

Because what really happened was ridiculous.

I holler upstairs, hoping to somehow avoid having to get off the couch. This never works.

So I push my things aside, stomp upstairs, and fling open the door. *Behold:*

One child hanging upside down from the bunk bed. Another boy straddling two beds, paused in mid-leap. And the smallest boy enjoying the show, absorbing

86

the example of his bigger brothers who know better – and this is what really goads me. *They know better.*

It's not just the boys. I know better, too, but here I am in all my fury. I turn off their light, assign extra chores for the morning, and huff downstairs. I'm out of answers and out of patience. And God's right there with me, of course – He's been right there all day long, but suddenly it's just us, minus the mayhem.

God is never maddened or exhausted with my questions, so I start asking some: What happened? Why do we end the day angry and out of sorts, when all I want to do is tuck them in and finish strong?

Sometimes I'm the one who requires endless amounts of correction and teaching.

Luke 6:45 says:

> *The good person out of the good treasure of his heart produces good, and the evil person out of his evil treasure produces evil, for out of the abundance of the heart his mouth speaks.*

And God says, *Talk to Me. Just like a little kid who talks to her parents incessantly, you need to talk to Me.*

He only calls us to speak to others the same way He speaks to us.

questions to consider:

- What does it look like to "put on" a compassionate heart, kindness, humility, meekness, and patience?
- What is God's tone when He speaks to you? What does this say about how He feels about you?
- How does the atmosphere around you change when you are talking to God?

(more) scripture for today:

> *Put on then, as God's chosen ones, holy and beloved, compassionate hearts, kindness, humility, meekness, and patience.*
>
> *- Colossians 3:12*

> *Preach the word; be ready in season and out of season; reprove, rebuke, and exhort, with complete patience and teaching.*
>
> *- 2 Timothy 4:2*

DAY 21

LIGHT

Our home, like yours maybe, has several work stations. The dining table doubles as a school desk, an ancient sideboard holds our computer, and the kitchen is often on duty from nine in the morning to well past midnight.

But there's one particular area that holds most of my affection. My family generously calls it "Mom's work table," although to be honest, there's almost no table to be seen underneath the mess of yarn and papers on top of it. Projects, craft stuff, books, a bazillion works in progress. Sometimes they even get finished.

But some days it all seems so trivial.

We hear about tragedy or discouraging events every day on the news, in Facebook, in our email alerts. We are bombarded with appeals to give, fund, call, sign, share, and do something about every single issue. Right now. Don't delay. Before it's too late. The times and the needs are urgent.

And they are. I know they are. But I just can't. We can't do it all, sign it all, share it all, or fund it all.

I feel this constant pull in two directions. On one side is the simplicity of building a happy home and nurturing beauty in a quiet life, but on the other side is an urgent feeling of the critical times we live in.

Maybe you're more balanced than I am, but I'm constantly asking God questions, like: When there are orphans needing families, people grieving, bodies hurting, and communities desperate for truth, why do I put so much time into the projects on my desk? What good is reading, writing, or creating artwork? For the love of all that is holy, why should we spend time painting, or playing music, or if we're going to be really honest, *steam cleaning the carpet,* when there is a culture to transform?

And God answered, *Because there **is** a culture to transform. That's exactly why. Your life and the details in it are a witness to others about My Kingdom. It's all ministry.*

God knows the joy in creating intricate detail, constructing beauty where before there was only ugliness and disorder. The same God who loves the orphan and heals the dying is also the Designer who made the finest veins on a leaf, the stripes on a housecat. God knows why we enjoy sewing stitches, composing music, and making paint strokes and key strokes.

We imitate our Father in the creator/designer aspect that is innovative and beautiful. We also reflect Him in the healer/redeemer role that is passionate, nurturing, world-changing, and in the trenches. And both sides are necessary.

Too much time focused on aesthetics leaves us aloof and ignorant, and too much time entrenched in warfare leaves us burned out and bitter.

But one more thing is needed to keep us in healthy equilibrium between the two. Without it, any light we attempt to create is blown out.

His presence is fire. Without it, no light. Our imitation of God is only a puff of hot air if we aren't actually spending time with Him.

Romans 12:21 says:

> *Do not be overcome by evil, but overcome evil with good.*

So we walk the path He calls us to – signing or singing, going or giving, praying, trusting, hoping, doing, waiting, sharing, learning, growing. Persevering. Triumphant. For the love of all that is holy.

Each gift we use from His presence is a fire.

Our culture sees Him by the light of it, and is transformed.

questions to consider:

- How are you seeing the culture and community around you transformed by the gifts God gives His people?
- How do your gifts bring light to the culture around you?
- What areas do you feel called to invest more time or prayer in? How can you make a step toward doing that today?

(more) scripture for today:

> *As for what was sown on good soil, this is the one who hears the word and understands it. He indeed bears fruit and yields, in one case a hundredfold, in another sixty, and in another thirty."*
>
> *- Matthew 13:23*
>
> *Keep your heart with all vigilance, for from it flow the springs of life.*
>
> *- Proverbs 4:23*

Notes

Day 3: Abiding

1. Hannah Whitall Smith, *The God of All Comfort* (Westwood, New Jersey: The Christian Library, 1984), 86.

Day 5: Identity

2. Louisa May Alcott, *Little Women* (Philadelphia, Penn: Running Press, 1995), 599.

Day 15: Friendship

3. Jane Austen, *Northanger Abbey* in *Jane Austen: The Complete Novels* (New York: Crown Publishers, Inc., 1981), 830.

CPSIA information can be obtained
at www.ICGtesting.com
Printed in the USA
LVHW021920040323
740852LV00003B/23